Solutions for Professional Learning Communities

How to Leverage PLCs for School Improvement

Sharon V. Kramer

Solution Tree | Press   a division of ▲ Solution Tree

555 North Morton Street
Bloomington, IN 47404
800.733.6786 (toll free) / 812.336.7700
FAX: 812.336.7790
email: info@solution-tree.com
solution-tree.com

Visit **go.solution-tree.com/PLCbooks** to download the reproducibles in this book.

Printed in the United States of America

19   18   17   16   15   1   2   3   4   5

Library of Congress Cataloging-in-Publication Data

Kramer, Sharon V.

How to leverage PLCs for school improvement / by Sharon V. Kramer.

    pages cm. -- (Solutions)

Includes bibliographical references.

    ISBN 978-1-936765-54-6 (perfect bound) 1. Professional learning communities--United States. 2. School improvement programs--United States. 3. Educational change--United States. I. Title.

LB1731.K73 2015

370.710973--dc23

                                 2015010153

Solution Tree
Jeffrey C. Jones, CEO
Edmund M. Ackerman, President

Solution Tree Press
President: Douglas M. Rife
Associate Acquisitions Editor: Kari Gillesse
Editorial Director: Lesley Bolton
Managing Production Editor: Caroline Weiss
Copy Editor: Ashante K. Thomas
Proofreader: Jessi Finn
Text and Cover Designer: Rian Anderson
Compositor: Abigail Bowen

Acknowledgments

I begin all my workshops and training sessions by stating that a professional learning community is as much about adult learning as it is about student learning. Because I believe this statement to be an absolute truth, I have been a student of the professional learning community framework for over twenty-five years. On my own journey, I have learned from educators across the United States and beyond. In every workshop, team meeting, classroom visit, and discussion with students, I learn something that causes me to reflect, ask questions, and think about how to improve options and opportunities for students. The challenges and the strategies and ideas to overcome them presented in this book are the result of what I have learned from these teachers, administrators, and students. I am forever grateful to them for allowing me to go along on their school-improvement journey.

The inspiration for this book is derived from the hard work and dedication of the U.S. Grant High School teachers and administrators who changed the lives of their students forever. These teachers put the students first and learned along with them. The students responded by persevering despite the long road with so many bumps along the way.

A special thank-you to Tamie Sanders, the former principal of U.S. Grant High School, who understood that the most important part of her job was to be a constant advocate for her students. Her unwavering focus changed not only the school culture but the very way the community viewed its school. She led the change at U.S. Grant from a "dropout factory to an engine of hope" for the students and community it serves.

I am also grateful to Cartwright School District in Arizona and Anoka-Hennepin School District in Minnesota for their work to improve their entire districts on a school-by-school basis. In addition, this work would not be possible without examples from Sanger Unified School District in California and the other schools and districts that have demonstrated evidence of effectiveness.

Most importantly, no one has had a greater impact on my work than the architects of Professional Learning Community at Work™, Richard DuFour, Robert Eaker, and Rebecca DuFour. Their work and efforts have given more hope to more students and educators than anything before or after them. The impact of PLCs has spanned the globe and at the same time touched the lives of individuals. My work and life have been so enriched because of my association with them.

Solution Tree, led by its visionary leader Jeffrey C. Jones, is the preeminent publishing and professional development company in the world. I am so grateful for the support, guidance, and belief in my work from the entire Solution Tree staff. I want to specifically thank Douglas M. Rife, Claudia Wheatley, and Shannon Ritz for their unwavering encouragement to write. This book would not have come to fruition without the editing and insights of Ashante K. Thomas and Kari Gillesse.

Finally, this work requires an enormous time commitment. I thank my husband, Craig, and my family for their understanding and belief in the importance of this work. I thank my grandchildren for being the inspiration and real reason to expend all the time and effort. This book is dedicated to them.

Visit **go.solution-tree.com/PLCbooks** to download the reproducibles in this book.

Table of Contents

About the Author

Sharon V. Kramer, PhD, knows firsthand the demands and rewards of working in a professional learning community (PLC). Sharon served as assistant superintendent for curriculum and instruction of Kildeer Countryside School District 96 in Buffalo Grove, Illinois. In this position, she ensured all students were prepared to enter Adlai E. Stevenson High School, a model PLC.

A seasoned educator, Sharon has taught in elementary, middle, and high school classrooms and served as a principal, a director of elementary education, an assistant superintendent, and a university professor. These experiences have shaped her commitment to learning for *all* students.

As a leader in the field, she emphasizes the importance of creating and using quality assessments as a continual part of the learning process. She has been referred to as an "educators' educator" by teachers, schools, and districts that she has partnered with. As an author, presenter, and educational coach, Sharon has been instrumental in improving schools across the United States from the ground up. She knows the unique challenges and opportunities educators who serve youth at risk face and offers practical solutions to these real-world problems.

Sharon earned a doctorate in educational leadership and policy studies from Loyola University of Chicago.

To learn more about Sharon's work, follow @DrKramer1 on Twitter.

To book Sharon V. Kramer for professional development, contact pd@solution -tree.com.

Introduction

Since 2001, the focus of school reform in the United States has been about turning around failing schools. The nation has not lacked for opinions, journal articles, media pundits, sponsored university research, state initiatives, and federal government approaches, or a never-ending list of things failing schools *should* do. All these areas focus on draconian accountability demands on teachers and principals. I would contend that the focus of these efforts is misguided.

U.S. Grant High School in Oklahoma City, Oklahoma, offers a different example. Grant's story begins and ends with students. Labeled a failing school for more than seven years by the state, Grant's turnaround is, at its heart, a story about what happens when students believe they *can* and *will* learn. Their story can be yours.

The culture and media surrounding Grant have been historically negative. The school has been called a "dropout factory" and "ground zero of education reform in Oklahoma" (The Oklahoman Editorial Board, 2012). According to the Oklahoma City Police Department, five of the six known gangs in Oklahoma City reside within the school-district boundaries. At the start of the 2011–2012 school year, 206 seniors (80 percent) had not met the state-testing requirements for graduation. Grant was placed on the Oklahoma State Department of Education's needs-improvement list for seven years in a row. The staff spent its time focusing on compliance, order, and safety instead of student achievement. During a 2010 board meeting, the Oklahoma City Public School Board designated Grant a Turnaround School and allocated additional funding through a school-improvement grant.

The School

U.S. Grant High School is the largest high school in Oklahoma City Public Schools, a multicultural district serving approximately forty-three thousand students. The following is a snapshot of Grant's demographic information.

- 123 teachers
- 1,640 students
- 98 percent of students receive free or reduced lunch

- 30 percent of students have limited English proficiency
- 15 percent of students are special education
- 12 percent are African American
- 70 percent are Hispanic
- 1 percent is Asian / Pacific Islander
- 10 percent are White
- 7 percent are Native American

A culture of failure existed that perpetuated itself year after year, fostering dropout after dropout. Under the leadership of principal Tamie Sanders, Grant began its journey of continuous improvement. She believed that creating a culture of success starts with believing it's possible. Any achievements in an organization are the results of the combined efforts of each individual. This includes the efforts of the students, teachers, administrators, and community supporters. Grant's situation was an opportunity to harness the power within.

A Reason to Celebrate

The State of Oklahoma administers seven end-of-instruction (EOI) exams that—along with course credits—determine eligibility for graduation. The exams occur in algebra 1 and 2, geometry, English 2 and 3, U.S. history, and biology. Students must pass algebra 1 and English 2 and at least two of the other tested courses. Prior to the 2011 school year, the pass rate for algebra 1 was zero percent since the school did not even test enough of the students to qualify. The new pass rate for algebra 1 was 91 percent in 2013. The other courses' pass rates have also increased dramatically. Table I.1 demonstrates the increase in the pass rate from 2012 to 2013 and then the cumulative pass rate over the three-year period from 2010 to 2013.

At the start of the 2011–2012 school year, 206 seniors (80 percent) had not met the state-testing requirements for graduation. By the end of the next school year, only four seniors (1.5 percent) had not met the state-testing requirements.

Other Indicators of Success

These impressive results are not the only indicators of success. According to Oklahoma's A–F Accountability System, U.S. Grant High School has moved from the bottom of the Fs to a B+, one point away from earning an A! Based on these results, National Math + Science Initiative (NMSI), Boeing, and the state's department of education awarded Grant $495,000 to offer advanced placement (AP) courses in mathematics, science, and English. Grant increased AP offerings in all core subject areas. Thirteen of the fifteen AP government students had qualifying scores on the test the first year the course was offered.

Table I.1: 2012–2013 and Overall Comparisons—Percent of Increase in Pass Rate

Course	2012 to 2013	2010 to 2013
English 2	+8 percent	+55 percent
English 3	+27 percent	+89 percent
Algebra 1	+12 percent	+295 percent
Geometry	+42 percent	+107 percent
Algebra 2	+145 percent	+523 percent
Biology	−41 percent	+82 percent
U.S. History	+38 percent	+116 percent

Principals and teachers might wonder, "Are there any other examples of schools that have improved and made a real difference for the students they serve?" The good news is yes! U.S. Grant High School is not unique. Other school districts demonstrating remarkable sustained improvement are Cartwright School District Number 83 in Arizona and Sanger Unified School District in California. Visit All Things PLC (www.allthingsplc.info) to read about these districts and to access additional examples of school turnaround from across the United States. Each of these schools has demonstrated effectiveness in improving student achievement using the professional learning community (PLC) model. The schools and districts described on All Things PLC vary in size, demographics, and poverty level. The one thing that they all have in common is that they made a commitment to learning for all and were willing to do whatever it takes to reach high levels of learning for all students. These improved achievement results were not just obtained for a single year but maintained over time. Each school and district approached this work as continuous improvement and has evidence over time that the PLC model is the right journey.

The Overwhelming Challenge

Everyone engaged in school improvement would agree that despite all the state and federal funding, education experiences, time, and energy, turning around a school is difficult work, and most schools lack the basic information needed to achieve success. No one disputes the challenges and high stakes of failing to improve. The question is always, How do schools and districts turn around? Principals and teachers are hardworking, dedicated individuals. It is not about hard work or lack of effort. It is about doing the right work that will result in learning for all students. School improvement really requires a commitment to learning for all students.

Why Should We Commit to Learning for All?

We must prepare students for their future, not our past. The students seated in the classrooms today are preparing for jobs and careers that have not been invented or imagined yet. Those students who have not learned how to learn will be left behind in the economy. As a nation in a global economy, we need to sustain access to the American Dream as the land of opportunity and social mobility. The gap in standardized test scores between affluent and low-income students has grown about 40 percent since the 1960s (Reardon, 2011). The imbalance between rich and poor students in college completion, the single most important predictor of success in the workforce, has grown 50 percent since the late 1980s. Education is the most powerful tool for helping students of poverty (Greenstone, Looney, Patashnik, & Yu, 2013). It is increasingly evident that the United States is falling behind the rest of the world. The United States dropped from first in the world in percentage of high school graduates to number twenty-two of twenty-seven advanced economies (The Broad Foundation, n.d.).

It is clear that our current systems and reform efforts are not working. Thirty percent of students who enter high school will drop out. Potential dropouts can be predicted as early as first grade and identified with accuracy by third grade (American Psychological Association, 2012; Sparks, 2013). Most importantly, there are serious implications for those who fail.

The implications for students who are unsuccessful in school are severe and life altering. U.S. dropouts are three times more likely to be unemployed and therefore more likely to live in poverty with an estimated annual salary of $20,241 (Breslow, 2012). They will earn thirty-three cents for every dollar a college graduate earns, and that constitutes the highest discrepancy in the world (Organisation for Economic Co-operation and Development, 2009; United States Census Bureau, 2006). Dropouts are more prone to ill health and are four times more likely to be uninsured. The most astonishing statistic is that the life expectancy for dropouts is an average of 10.5 fewer years for women and 13 years for men than those with a high school diploma (Tavernise, 2012). Dropouts are sixty-three times more likely to be incarcerated at a cost of $292,000 over their lifetime (Breslow, 2012).

The most important reason to commit to learning for all is because teachers want to be the best they can for the students they serve. Students count on them, and they step up every day to meet those expectations. Educators understand the moral imperative they have to provide the same quality education for their students that they would want for their own children, grandchildren, and other family members. School improvement is, at its heart, a story about what happens when teachers and principals help students believe they *can* and *will* learn. This student-centered approach is exactly what improves schools.

Finally, a school or district must commit to learning for all to improve student achievement. Without a focused, laser-sharp commitment to learning for all students, a school or district will make small gains at best. In the worst-case scenario, teachers and administrators work extremely hard to find that student achievement actually regresses. School improvement is not only about working hard. The schools, districts, and teacher teams must work on the *right work*.

About This Book

The question is, What is the right work? This book demonstrates how leveraging the power of professional learning communities is the right work. Specific challenges to school improvement are the focus with solutions and strategies. School improvement requires shifts in current practices, specifically a shift to a culture of collaboration, a shift to determining and addressing the specific needs of each student, and a shift to leadership for learning. Each section ends with reflection questions and implications for schools. The challenges to school improvement are summarized in the epilogue, and schools are encouraged to create a Start Doing–Stop Doing list (figure E.1, page 58) that captures key points and obstacles to school improvement that must be addressed to move their improvement process forward.

Tamie Sanders, principal of U.S. Grant High School, hung a sign in the office as the school began its PLC journey. It read: How hard can it be? Later she wrote: Really, really hard! As that year progressed, a teacher came by and wrote: But so worth it!

Chapter 1
First Challenge: Creating a Culture of Success

Optimism is the faith that leads to achievement; nothing can be done without hope and confidence.

—Helen Keller

Schools are rated and ranked with a variety of designations. Some states use a letter-grade system while others use designations like reward, priority, or focus schools. No matter what system is used, it is clear that the ratings are very public. Realtors sell houses based on school rankings. Communities advertise school results to attract businesses and families to their areas. Parents select schools and districts based on these designations. Worst of all, students are acutely aware when their school is underperforming. They often come to school with a "why-try" attitude.

The greatest challenge to school improvement is the overwhelming perception that no matter what the teachers and administrators do, there seems to be no way out of failing results. With some of the lowest annual student-achievement results, there is a perception among staff that students' poverty and low skills, as well as disengaged families, are more potent than any teacher's impact, which leads to a sense of futility. Teachers often feel deflated by a sense that their best efforts are ineffective and unappreciated by students, families, or the system in which they work.

When these circumstances persist over years, a culture of failure exists that is difficult to overcome. No number of structures can surmount this overwhelming perception that failure describes us. Schools attempt to fix the problems by adopting new curricula or textbooks, revising the schedule, or implementing a new discipline program. But while these structural changes may be necessary, they are never enough to overcome a culture of failure. Culture always trumps structure.

Building Collective Responsibility for Student Learning

Schools that implement the professional learning community model of continuous improvement accept learning as their fundamental purpose. Because they believe and commit to this learning focus, they are willing to examine all their practices in light of their impact on student learning. This means all practices, like schedules, grading, homework, assessment, and interventions—not just the ones that are easily agreed on or changed.

Schools build a culture focused on learning. A learning-focused culture requires that teachers commit to two fundamental assumptions: (1) all students can learn at high levels (grade level or better), and (2) educators accept responsibility to ensure high levels of learning for every student. As educators, we profess to believe all students can learn, but we often add a qualifier: "All students can learn if they are not in special education." "All students can learn if their first language is English." "All students can learn if they have supportive, involved parents." "All students can learn if they do their homework." "All students can learn if they can read at grade level."

It is hard to ignore the variables that we cannot control. These are the factors that impact learning that teachers and principals really cannot change. Some schools and teams spend a great deal of time focusing on the problems that they cannot control or influence. This is like looking out the schoolhouse window and hoping that the right students show up or that the parents suddenly become more involved. In schools, we need to teach the students who show up, not the ones we thought were coming or we wish were coming. Schools that truly want to improve focus their time and attention on variables they can control (see figure 1.1). In other words, instead of spending time looking out the window, they look in the mirror and ask what is possible for the students who attend their school. What can they do to ensure that all students learn?

As educators, parents entrust us with the most important and precious thing in their lives—their children. They trust that we will keep them safe, make them feel accepted and special, and ensure that they learn. So once again, the questions remain: Do we agree all students can learn at high levels? To what extent do we accept responsibility to ensure that all students are learning?

Uncontrollable Variables	Controllable Variables
Children cannot choose: • Their parents • Where they live • The school they attend • Their teachers • The high-stakes summative assessments they'll take	Collaborative teacher teams can develop: • A school and classroom culture of caring and encouragement • A guaranteed, viable curriculum • Effective, research-based teaching strategies • Common formative assessments of student learning • Systems of providing additional time, support, and enrichment • Ways to frequently recognize and celebrate improvement

Source: Eaker & Keating, 2012, p. 9. Used with permission.

Figure 1.1: Impacting student learning in a professional learning community.

School improvement requires an unwavering focus on learning. Schools that realize the most gains in achievement rally the entire staff around the singular mission *learning for all.* They limit the initiatives in order to focus all their time and attention on being a professional learning community. Improving schools realize that if they do the *right work* of a professional learning community, achievement improves, and they are actually incorporating the research-based, high-leverage strategies and initiatives that have the greatest impact on student learning. Improving schools understand the need to become a PLC focused on student learning.

Shifting the Culture

Culture consists of the norms, values, beliefs, ceremonies, symbols, and stories that we tell each other about our work, our students, and our school or district. In order to improve, schools need to create and tell a different story. What are the positive things that define our work, our students, and our school? Celebrate quick wins no matter how small they may seem. Moving students in and out of interventions is a win. Passing a short formative quiz is a win. Demonstrating growth in any class or subject is a win. More students completing their work is a win. Celebrating any and all small victories is the only way to turn the tide. Changing the culture requires all of us to tell a different story about our school. It begins by communicating these small victories widely. Teachers and students must create a sense that success is inevitable, attainable, and irresistible!

This cultural shift begins by adopting specific core principles that guide the work and set the tone for school improvement.

1. Do not blame the students.
2. Learning is required.
3. Hope is not a strategy.

Administrators and teachers alike consciously act on these principles.

In most schools, the easiest answer to failure is to blame the students. The more difficult task is to examine all practices, policies, and procedures that may be getting in the way of student learning. Many of the current practices in schools are done just because schools always have done them that way. Improving schools are willing to review and change these in light of their effect on learning. They change what needs changing now, not next year or next semester. All the changes are based on student needs. In some instances, this means changing teacher assignments and student schedules. Improving schools are willing to act flexibly and strategically in making midstride corrections along the way.

"Learning is required here—not optional" is the mantra of improving schools. They do not invite learning to occur. They require that students, teachers, and administrators learn together. For example, students may not opt out of learning by refusing to turn in assignments and taking a zero. Rather, students are required to attend a lunch study hall to complete the work instead of eating with their friends.

Learning is also required of the teachers and administrators. The entire school builds shared knowledge around the work of collaborative teams and PLCs. This learning does not come from a year or two of study at workshops or by merely doing book studies. Improving schools take a learning by doing approach. In other words, they start doing before they have all the answers or understand the process perfectly. Teams are encouraged to "fail forward" using the knowledge they gain by actually engaging in the work. There is a sense of urgency that prevails in all they do. This urgency underlines the need to help the students now, not later. Schools understand that by the time all teachers and staff learn enough to be totally comfortable, more students will have already failed. The time is now.

Hope is not a strategy for improvement. Some schools do exactly what they have done year after year and hope for a different result. Hope is a wish, not an action that will result in more learning for students. Teachers and teams must do more than hope for better results. They need to use data to impact instruction on a daily basis. They must be flexible and willing to do whatever it takes to get better results for their students, even if it means changing schedules, disrupting the routine, or slowing down instruction to scaffold up the learning. What teachers do each and every day matters. Actions directly linked to more learning for students must be identified and implemented. This strategy is much more powerful than hope alone.

Reflection and Next Steps

Use the following questions to help your team reflect and consider your next steps.

1. How can our school shift from a culture of failure to one of hope for students, staff, and parents? How can our school or district overcome a cycle of failure?

2. If we are to become the school committed to *learning for all*, what would be required of us as teachers and administrators?

3. What commitments would we have to make and observe to create this kind of school? What schoolwide commitments would we need to make in the areas of curriculum, assessment, instruction, interventions, grading, and student learning?

Chapter 2

Second Challenge: Engaging in the Right Work

Classrooms, schools, and school systems can and do improve, and the factors facilitating improvement are neither so exotic, unusual, or expensive that they are beyond the grasp of ordinary schools.

—David Clark, Linda Lotto, and Terry Astuto

What is the right work? What are the necessary conditions for all learners to succeed? What are the high-leverage elements that have the greatest impact on learning? It turns out that the right work does not require superhuman powers. It requires the ability to harness the power within a school. The professional learning community model is the organizing structure or framework that harnesses the power within to improve schools: "Our primary assumption is that the professional learning community model offers our best hope for ensuring high levels of learning for all students" (Eaker & Keating, 2012, p. 8).

The quantitative and qualitative research on PLCs' positive effects on school improvement are well documented in the literature and on All Things PLC (www .allthingsplc.info). (Visit the section "Articles and Research" at www.allthingsplc .info to read specific accounts of school-improvement efforts.) Educational organizations and educational researchers alike endorse and embrace PLC concepts. The PLC framework has swept North America and is making a global impact. So what is a PLC? According to experts Richard DuFour, Rebecca DuFour, Robert Eaker, and Thomas Many (2010):

> [A professional learning community] is an ongoing process in which educators work collaboratively in recurring cycles of collective inquiry and action research to achieve better results for the students they serve. Professional learning communities operate under the assumption that the key to improved learning for students is continuous, job-embedded learning for educators. (p. 11)

Professional learning communities are not a new program or a meeting or a book study or a checklist. Instead, acting as a professional learning community is a way of being. Teachers and teams have described it as the way they work together to ensure all students are learning. It is a continuous-improvement model that, when implemented with fidelity, results in high levels of learning for all students. *If you build it, they will learn.*

A PLC focuses on three big ideas that drive improvement efforts. The first big idea is the unwavering focus on student learning. Most often, schools focus on teaching, not learning. Consider this: Teachers spend a great deal of time composing lesson plans. They often include technology and a constructivist approach to instruction utilizing manipulatives and engaging activities in these plans to make them as effective as possible. The problem is this: if, as a result of the lesson, the students have not learned, then all the planning really doesn't matter. The shift must be to focus on what students have learned, not just what unit or lesson the teacher is teaching that day. This seems like a small shift, but as teachers, we have always focused much of our time and energy on producing lesson plans and designing activities. This is exactly how we were all trained as educators. Teachers who are focused on learning rather than teaching do quick checks for understanding as each new concept is taught and use this information to redirect the lesson or students to ensure learning occurs. This happens during the lesson, and it serves as immediate feedback to the students and teacher. The shift is from what is being taught to what students actually learn.

The second big idea is that the adults must work together collaboratively in order to ensure that students will learn. No one individual has all the knowledge or skills to meet the varying needs of students. This requires a collective effort.

The third big idea is a focus on results. In the end, all the activity or action plans that are developed and implemented must result in the anticipated improvement in student achievement. Concrete results, rather than just good intentions, must determine the effectiveness of any effort.

Shifting to a Culture of Collaboration

"Where should we begin?" and "What should we do first t   schools?" are questions schools ask when they realize the need is great and time is limited. There is a sense of urgency to improve, but often, the structures are not in place to support high levels of learning. The first step is to establish collaborative teams: "Great schools row as one; they are quite clearly in the same boat, pulling in the same direction in unison. The best schools we visited were tightly aligned communities marked by a palpable sense of we" (Lickona & Davidson, 2005, p. 65). In a professional learning community, no one works in isolation. Teams can be structured in a variety of ways depending on the configuration and size of the school. Six possible team structures include:

1. All teachers teaching the same grade level

2. All teachers teaching the same course

3. Logical combinations of teachers with similar responsibilities

4. Vertical teams of teachers (K–2, 3–5, 6–8 mathematics, or German levels 1–4)

5. District or regional teams

6. Electronic teams that collaborate and share information via technology

Many schools respond by stating that they have worked in teams for years, so what else should they do? This question rings especially true for middle schools. The middle school philosophy includes the establishment of grade-level teams that share the same students. However, the act of meeting together does not define a group of people as a team. The most important questions that distinguish a team from a group are these: Are the members of the team working collaboratively? Are they focused on the right work? Does each team have a goal that it is mutually accountable to achieve? The definition of a team is educators who work interdependently to accomplish a common goal for which they are mutually accountable. Team goals are focused on ensuring high levels of learning for all students. The expectation is that teams will collaborate and monitor these goals to obtain better results for the students they serve.

Collaborative teams are the engine that drives school improvement. Collaboration is as much about adult learning as it is about student learning. Teachers improve their practice when they collaborate. Consider this: no matter how good a teacher is, no matter how much knowledge or skill he or she has as an individual, the students are limited by what that one person brings to that lesson or activity. When a teacher works on a team, the options and opportunities for students grow exponentially.

So what does it mean to collaborate? Collaboration is "a *systematic process* in which [teams] work together, interdependently, to analyze and *impact* their professional practice in order to improve their individual and collective results" (DuFour, DuFour, Eaker, & Many, 2010, p. 120). True collaboration requires that systems and structures exist to ensure that teams are focused on learning. The goal is to build highly effective and efficient self-directed collaborative teams. This requires clearly established expectations and time lines that describe the work and products that are a result of team members' collaborative efforts. Figure 2.1 describes the expectations and guides the work of teams. It is divided into five sections. Section one sets the expectations for the collaborative work of teams, and sections two through five (PLC questions 1–4) describe the actual work of the team.

Collaborative team time must be built into the regular daily schedule or occur at least weekly. Collaboration cannot occur outside the school day. Teams need ongoing professional development and support as they work. Administrators need to support the work by attending meetings, designating team facilitators, or both. The administrators and team facilitators serve as coaches to the team. Their role is not to do all the work for the team. The intent is to build the capacity of the team to "co-labor" together. Teams often struggle at first or encounter challenges along the way, so each team may need a different set of supports to move forward. Differentiated just-in-time professional development may be required on a team-by-team basis. This differentiated support and coaching has proved to be most beneficial because it is targeted to the specific needs of each team and moves the process forward in a timely manner.

Collaborative team time is not an opportunity to discuss field trips, dress-code issues, students who are tardy or absent, or other procedural things. Collaborative teamwork must have a direct impact on what happens in classrooms. This means that collaborative team meetings focus on curriculum, instruction, assessment, and data that drive student interventions. Often teams meet and discuss student learning, but nothing changes as a result of their meeting. The intent of true collaboration is to impact instructional and curricular practices in a way that improves student learning. In other words, teams must be focused on the *right work*.

The right work of teams focuses on answering these four critical PLC questions on a unit-by-unit basis (DuFour, DuFour, Eaker, & Many, 2010).

1. What is it we expect students to know and be able to do?
2. How will we know when they have learned?
3. How will we respond when they do not learn?
4. How will we respond when they already know it?

Question one is foundational and requires teams to identify the essential standards for each unit they teach. Teams clarify essential leanings (skills, knowledge,

Defined Tasks for Collaborative Teams	Completion Date	Products or Artifacts
Create and monitor team norms.		Norms
Establish protocols: roles, agenda building, record keeping, consensus, and so on.		Protocols
Establish team SMART goals.		SMART goals
Continuously monitor progress on SMART goals using summative and common formative assessments.		SMART goal action plan
Celebrate success, including small wins along the way!		Description of celebrations (include recipients, dates, and times)
PLC Question 1: What do we expect our students to know and be able to do?		
Review state standards and align curriculum.		Curriculum documents
Identify the essential standards for each grade level or subject area using endurance, leverage, and readiness criteria.		List of essential grade-level or content-specific standards

Continued ↓

Figure 2.1: PLC products, tasks, and time lines.

Defined Tasks for Collaborative Teams	Completion Date	Products or Artifacts
PLC Question 1: What is it we expect students to know and be able to do?		
Vertically align essential standards looking for gaps and redundancies.		Aligned curriculum guides
Pace the curriculum with emphasis on when the learning targets will be taught.		Pacing guide or course sequence
PLC Question 2: How will we know when they have learned?		
Unwrap each of the essential standards into learning targets. (Determine learning progression.)		Unwrapped essential standards with learning targets
Map each standard indicating the summative and formative assessments.		Assessment map for each essential standard
Develop common formative assessments for each learning target.		Common formative assessments
Determine proficiency levels.		Rationale
Develop grading rubric or scoring guide.		Rubric or written criteria

Defined Tasks for Collaborative Teams	Completion Date	Products or Artifacts
PLC Question 2: How will we know if they've learned it?		
Write learning targets in student-friendly language by engaging students in the process.		Student-friendly targets
Create and share anchor papers with students demonstrating strong and weak work. (Collaboratively score student work.)		Anchor papers
Analyze assessment results.		Item analysis, data-team protocol, or both
PLC Question 3: How will we respond when they do not learn?		
Identify systematic responses for students who are failing.		Remediation strategies
Create interventions for students who fail to meet learning targets on common formative assessments.		Intervention strategies
Identify students for interventions by essential standard or learning target and specific need.		List of students with specific data

Continued →

Defined Tasks for Collaborative Teams	Completion Date	Products or Artifacts
PLC Question 3: How will we respond when they do not learn?		
Group students for instruction by specific essential standard, learning target, or need.		Student groupings by essential standard, learning target, or need
Evaluate the progress of students after interventions.		Monitoring tool
PLC Question 4: How will we respond when they already know it?		
Identify systematic responses for students who have already mastered the essential standards.		Student groupings by standard, learning target, or need
Create extension activities for students who demonstrate proficiency and better.		Extension activities
Identify students who demonstrate proficiency and better on common formative assessments.		List of students with specific data
Evaluate the progress of students after the extension activity.		Monitoring tool

*Visit **go.solution-tree.com/PLCbooks** for a reproducible version of this figure.*

concepts, dispositions) for each course or subject to ensure students have access to a guaranteed and viable curriculum. According to Robert Marzano (2003), creating a guaranteed and viable curriculum is the number-one factor for increased levels of learning. A guaranteed curriculum means that no matter which teacher a student is assigned, the curriculum will be the same. In other words, what students learn in fifth-grade science will be the same content no matter who teaches the class. A viable curriculum means that teachers can actually teach and students can learn the essential standards in the time allotted.

Teachers are quick to state that there is too much to teach! They are absolutely correct. Marzano supports this assertion in his analysis of standards and time. He states, "To cover all of this content, you would have to change schooling from K–12 to K–22. . . . The sheer number of standards is the biggest impediment to implementing standards" (Scherer, 2001, p. 15). Although they are more targeted, the Common Core standards and other new or revised state standards are far too many to learn in a school year. Teams must collaborate to determine which of the standards are essential from those that are nice to know or peripheral. Essential standards do not represent all that teachers teach. They represent the minimum a student must learn to reach high levels of learning. They serve to establish the focus for assessing student learning and implementing interventions when students do not learn. Teachers are not creating a list but building shared knowledge of what the most important skills, concepts, and understandings are that will result in higher levels of achievement. This is about focus, focus, focus.

The most efficient process for determining which standards are essential, or priority standards, is to apply the three criteria Larry Ainsworth (2003a) describes in his book *Power Standards: Identifying the Standards That Matter the Most*: (1) endurance, (2) leverage, and (3) readiness. (See figure 2.2, page 22.)

Teams begin to clarify what it is students really need to know and be able to do by answering two questions collaboratively: (1) What does this standard mean, and (2) What would it look like if a student could actually do what the standard requires? In other words, they must agree on what proficiency really means. To truly understand proficiency, teams rely on test specifications with content limits, blueprints, and released-test items from state and national tests to determine the depth of knowledge or thinking levels that each student needs to engage in to be proficient or master the standard.

Teachers rarely teach an entire standard or outcome at one time or in one lesson. Instead, teams unwrap standards into smaller learning targets to determine the learning progression on the path to mastery of the essential standard. These smaller parts that underpin an essential standard become the basis for daily instruction, formative assessment, and interventions. For example, figure 2.3 (page 23) includes an essential standard with three separate learning targets.

Endurance: Knowledge and skills of value beyond a single test date. Will the standard be employed exactly as it is in life beyond the school walls? Does it represent how things are really done?

Leverage: Knowledge and skills of value in multiple disciplines. Is the standard transferable and even necessary for learners to access skills and content in other areas or fields?

Readiness: Knowledge and skills necessary for success in the next grade level, the next instruction level, or the state test. Is the standard a building block that other standards are contingent on?

Essential Standards Protocol

Collaborative teams use these criteria to identify seven to twelve or approximately one-third of the state standards per subject or per grade level.

1. Individual teachers decide the absolutely essential standards using the endurance, leverage, and readiness criteria.
2. Teams discuss and reach consensus on the essential standards.
3. Teams consult testing information to determine alignment (test specifications, blueprints, or content limits).
4. Teams record selected standards.
5. Teams check for redundancies and gaps from course to course or grade level to grade level.

Source: Adapted from Ainsworth, 2003a.

Figure 2.2: Essential standards criteria.
*Visit **go.solution-tree.com/PLCbooks** for a reproducible version of this figure.*

A guaranteed and viable curriculum is accomplished only when teachers who are called on to teach the curriculum work collaboratively to study the intended curriculum and agree on priorities within it. Each team clarifies exactly how the curriculum translates into specific student knowledge and skills and establishes pacing guidelines. Finally, team members make a commitment to each other that they will actually teach the curriculum.

Often teachers believe prioritizing and unwrapping the standards are the district office's work or that they have already been done for them because they have state standards. This belief is validated when the district or state department sends out pacing guides and other related materials. Small teams of teachers often develop these curriculum documents and then distribute them to everyone. Unfortunately, the only teachers who truly understand these resources are the ones who participated in creating them. Everyone else spends time trying to understand and make sense of this information. This is because the thinking that occurred to develop those resources is

---

Essential Standard: Trace and evaluate the argument and specific claims in an informational text, distinguishing claims that are supported by reasons and evidence from those that are not. (NGA & CCSSO, 2010; RI.6.8)

Learning Targets

1. Trace the argument and specific claims in informational text.

2. Evaluate the argument and specific claims in informational text.

3. Distinguish claims that are supported from those that are not.

Teams work collaboratively to unwrap the essential standards into separate learning targets using the protocol outlined below. It is best to do this before each new unit of instruction begins. This process ensures that teachers begin instruction with a clear understanding of the targets. Lesson planning is facilitated by the discussion team members have during the unwrapping process.

Protocol for Unwrapping Standards

To find the learning targets to teach and assess, teams must:

1. Circle the verbs (skills).

2. Underline the nouns (concepts) to be taught.

3. Double underline any prepositional phrase (context).

4. Write separately each verb (skill) and noun (concept) combination as a separate learning target.

5. If a prepositional phrase (context) is included at the beginning or the end of the standard, include it in the target.

6. Examine each learning target, asking the following questions—

   ○ What are the instructional and assessment implications of this target?

   ○ What would it look like to teach this target in the classroom (setting, materials, strategies)?

   ○ Is the skill measurable? What would the assessment look like? Do we need to change the verb to make it more measurable?

7. After examining the instructional and assessment implications, are there any targets that are implicit or not directly stated in the standard that should be included?

Source: Adapted from Bailey & Jakicic, 2012.

Figure 2.3: Example of unwrapped standard.
*Visit **go.solution-tree.com/PLCbooks** for a reproducible version of this figure.*

more important than the resources themselves. The fact that you have state standards and district-curriculum guides does not ensure that individual teacher teams have a shared understanding of the standards and learning targets that they are expected to teach. Teachers must be masters of the standards they teach. Determining the most essential standards for your students, unwrapping them to find the learning targets that underpin them, and agreeing on proficiency levels is the way teams and individual teachers become masters of the standards they teach. Once teams have a shared understanding of what students will learn, they are ready to answer PLC question two: How will we know when students have learned?

The lynchpin of the collaborative team process is the implementation of common assessments. An assessment is common if it is the same assessment administered at the same time by two or more teachers who teach the same content. The purpose of common assessments is to identify (1) which students did not demonstrate mastery of essential learning targets and standards, (2) effective instructional practices, and (3) patterns in student errors and misconceptions. In addition, teams measure the accuracy of the assessment items. Most importantly, teams plan and target intervention efforts based on these results.

Unfortunately, many times the only assessments that are administered are summative end-of-unit or semester exams. Their intended use is to merely assign a grade. These assessments are used to measure learning, not diagnose and intervene. Because their purpose is different than formative assessments', teachers often assign a grade and move on.

The research is clear that the most powerful strategy to improve student learning is the use of formative assessments aligned to summative assessments (Black, Harrison, Marshall, & Wiliam, 2003; Black & Wiliam, 1998; Wiliam, Lee, Harrison, & Black, 2004). Formative assessments inform learning by diagnosing specific needs so that teachers and students know exactly what a student has learned, and they can respond in a targeted and timely manner. Formative assessments can take almost any form as a concept is taught, such as a quick check for understanding—for example, short quizzes, exit tickets, or any other activities that serve to guide instruction and let the student know what he or she has learned and what he or she still needs to learn. It is a process that ensures learning for all students by not allowing them to get lost or behind.

The closer the assessment and intervention are to first instruction, the greater the learning. The purpose of formative assessment is to use the information and data to help students learn more. The information from these assessments assists teams in answering PLC questions three and four: How will we respond when students do not learn, and How will we respond when they already know it? Formative assessments are often not graded because they represent student practice in learning a skill or concept on the way to mastery.

The way teachers and students use information from the assessment determines whether it is formative or summative. Ask the following questions to determine if an assessment is formative.

- Is the assessment used to find students who need more time and support to learn? Is the assessment used to find students who have already learned the standards?

- Do the students who have not learned yet receive additional time, support, and instruction to demonstrate their learning? Do the students who have already learned receive an extension of their learning, not more of the same? Then, are these same students also given an opportunity to demonstrate their new knowledge?

- Are teams using the information from common formative assessments to target interventions and extensions of the learning for the identified students?

Two strategies are proven to be most effective in increasing student learning: (1) the administering of common formative assessments and (2) the discussion of their results as a team. According to Connie Moss and Susan Brookhart (2009), the common formative assessment process is "lightning in a bottle" (p. 23): "In a very real way it flips a switch, shining a bright light on individual teaching decisions so that teachers can see clearly (perhaps for the first time) the difference between the intent and the effect of their actions" (p. 10). The process has the following benefits:

- It costs nothing.

- It works in every classroom, grade level, and subject area.

- It works each minute of every school day.

- It increases learning for all students.

- It raises teacher quality.

- It forges learning partnerships between students and teachers.

In a professional learning community, common formative assessments are the pathway for teachers to analyze and improve their practice. This is truly job-embedded professional development. As teams work collaboratively to write, administer, and analyze the results of assessments to intervene and extend the learning for their students, teachers are also learning the most powerful instructional strategies that will increase learning for their students. Figure 2.4 (page 26) contains the actions and activities a team engages in as it answers the critical questions and also describes the nonPLC response.

1. What is it we expect students to know and be able to do?	
PLC Actions	**NonPLC Actions**
• Prioritize standards. • Group standards into units. Determine when proficiency with each is expected. • Develop scope and sequence (pacing). • Unpack standards to understand the learning targets and write student-friendly learning targets. • Determine rigor needed for proficiency of learning. • Identify practices or processes students need to learn with the content standards.	• Group standards arbitrarily or spontaneously and teach without a plan or with a minimal plan. • Agree on a few standards, and individuals choose the rest. • Use a book as a guide for what to teach and when to teach over standards. • Agree to disagree on the level of rigor needed to demonstrate proficiency. • Teach standards in isolation. • Individually interpret the meaning of standards.
2. How will we know when they have learned?	
PLC Actions	**NonPLC Actions**
• Create and use common formative and summative assessments. • Use common scoring guides and rubrics to assess student learning on common assessments. • Calibrate scoring of common assessments. • Analyze data from common assessments and respond. • Identify trends in student work and respond. • Identify and plan for classroom formative assessment processes in daily lessons.	• Give independently teacher-created assessments to one's own class. • Agree on only some common items and leave freedom for teachers to independently choose the remaining items. • Score assessments independently. • Analyze data without a response (move on). • Give tests on different days. • Only give students feedback on unit assessments, ignoring formative assessment in daily instruction or vice versa.

3. How will we respond when they do not learn?	
PLC Actions	**NonPLC Actions**
• Look at trends in student work and re-engage all learners. • Re-engage all learners without lowering the cognitive demand of the target or standard as needed. • Accelerate learning so students can access grade-level standards. • Base decisions on data, not a student's education label. • Create a systematic pyramid of interventions to meet the needs of all learners.	• Focus solely on basic skills. • Slow down and stretch content without accelerating learning and including grade-level content. • Group students based on education label rather than academic ability. • Change (lower) expectations for student proficiency. • Reteach the same concept in a similar way or with lower expectations.
4. How will we respond when they already know it?	
PLC Actions	**NonPLC Actions**
• Look at trends in student work and re-engage all learners. • Re-engage learners and deepen their understanding of a target or standard rather than skim future grade-level content. • Raise text complexity, if appropriate. • Base decisions on data, not a student's education label. • Honor and advance student learning.	• Give students more difficult problems or activities. • Speed through content to cover more or future content. • Group students based on education label (gifted and talented education, English language learner, and so on) rather than ability. • Change (raise) expectations for student proficiency. • Reteach the same concept after it is learned. • Require students to always help or teach others.

Source: Adapted from Sarah Schuhl, 2014. Used with permission.

Figure 2.4: PLC and nonPLC responses to student learning.

Reflection and Next Steps

Use the following questions to help your team reflect and consider your next steps.

1. Are our school and teams engaged in the right work?

2. Does a culture of collaboration exist at our school? What needs to be in place to support the work of collaborative teams?

3. How can we ensure a focus on results?

4. Clarity always precedes competency in the teams' work. Use the information in figure 2.4 (page 27) to determine what our collaborative teams need to stop doing, start doing, or continue doing to ensure they are engaged in the right work.

Chapter 3
Third Challenge: Shifting From All to Each

Every student can learn, just not on the same day, or in the same way.

—George Evans

We have data, now what? Schools usually have an overwhelming amount of data and information about their students, but unfortunately, most of it does little to improve student achievement. Turning data into usable information that can be acted on in a timely manner is what improves schools. Data that move learning forward are linked to a specific standard, learning target, and student need.

Schools spend an inordinate amount of time analyzing their state-test data. Although necessary and helpful in calibrating curriculum, the instructional program, and alignment to the state standards, it rarely can be used to target specific student needs. The most valuable data are those derived from common formative and summative assessments. This information informs instruction on a daily, weekly, and monthly basis. Some teams declare, "We do common assessments." When asked what they do with the data from these assessments, the response is usually vague. Improving student achievement is not about writing the common assessment, scoring it, or merely examining the date; it is really about what happens next.

The specific manner in which teams respond to the data is what moves the learning forward. In order to take action that impacts student achievement based on the information gathered from the data, teams must examine each individual standard or learning target. Merely calculating the class average score on an assessment does not allow you to see the entire picture and certainly does not focus on the needs of individual students. Consider this: A collaborative team administers a common assessment and discusses the results. As team members look at the information, they determine that one of the classes has an average score of 72 percent. Since 70 percent is passing, the team comments that the students made significant progress. However, this average score is misleading, because as the team looks further into the data, they find that only three of the thirty-two students have a passing score! This information provides a very different picture of how well the students are progressing than the average score of the class.

Improving schools focus their attention on student progress, not group progress. As teams review the data from a common assessment, discussion progresses through the following questions.

1. **On which essential standards or learning targets did students perform the lowest?** Teams review the errors of the most often missed items to determine the misconceptions or reasons for the errors. They discuss which strategies teammates whose students performed well used.

2. **Based on the team discussion, what is the plan for improving the results?** Be specific. Responses should include more detail than "reteach," "remediate," "go over the test items," and so on.

3. **Which of the students need additional time and support to achieve at or above proficiency on the standards or learning targets?** Teams include specific standards or learning targets with each student's name.

4. **What is the team's plan to extend the learning for students who are highly proficient?** Be specific. Responses should include more detail than an additional assignment. What specific task will students be assigned that honors and extends their learning?

Collaborative teams utilize the following protocol (figure 3.1) to answer these questions. (Visit **go.solution-tree.com/PLCbooks** to download a reproducible version of this figure.)

This comprehensive analysis of data derived from common assessments will ensure that more students are proficient and are keeping up with the pace of the curriculum. It also identifies specific teaching strategies that worked and should be replicated.

Intervention and Remediation

In his presentations, PLC expert Richard DuFour often says, "Don't tell me you believe 'all students can learn' . . . tell me what you're doing about the kids who aren't learning." One of the greatest challenges that teachers face daily is responding to the academic diversity in their classrooms. Because academic diversity in many classrooms is so great, school-improvement efforts must focus on both intervention and remediation. It is often the case that some students can be as many as two to three years below grade level in reading or mathematics. These students are at a huge disadvantage because they are struggling to keep up in their current grade without many of the necessary prerequisite skills. Often in the traditional teach-and-test cycle, these students understand some of what has been taught but not all the important skills and concepts. After the test, the teacher needs to move on to finish the required curriculum. As teachers move on to the next unit, they try to spend time reteaching the concepts that were not learned. This traditional approach is not only difficult for teachers to manage and pace, it is also detrimental to students. Consider this: What is the likelihood that the students who failed to learn the first time will be able to relearn the essential standards from the previous unit while simultaneously keeping up in the next unit? The answer is unlikely. These students get into a cycle of remediation that is impossible to escape. As the year progresses, they get further and further behind. When this happens over multiple years, students give up.

Each teacher must fill in his or her data prior to the meeting and bring the completed form to the team meeting.

Team: _____   Teacher: _____   Date: _____

Common assessment: _____

The following analysis is based on the team's common assessment of the following standards or learning targets.

    1. _____

    2. _____

    3. _____

---

1. On which essential standards or learning targets did students perform the lowest? Discuss what strategies the teammates whose students performed well used.

Teachers	Strategies Used	Overall Pass Rate

Continued →

Source: Adapted from DuFour, 2011.

Figure 3.1: Sample data analysis protocol.

2. Based on the team discussion, what is the plan for improving the results? Be specific. Responses should include more detail than "reteach," "remediate," and so on.

Standard	Plan for Improving Results

3. Which of the students need additional time and support to achieve at or above proficiency on the standards or learning targets? Include the specific standards or learning targets with each student's name.

Student Name	Standards or Learning Targets Not Met	Plan for Intervention

4. What is the team's plan to extend the learning for students who are highly proficient? Be specific.

Student Name	Standards Mastered	Plan for Enrichment

How can these students catch up? These students need both remediation and intervention. What's the difference between remediation and intervention? Remediation includes actions to reverse established patterns of achievement by students who *already* are struggling or failing and who need intensive, long-term help. Supplemental instruction focuses on content that students should have mastered but have not. Intervention is a plan of action the teacher implements for students who need extra help or acceleration. These students are typically in the early stages of difficulties. Interventions are intended to address weaknesses *before* they become a problem (National Council of Teachers of Mathematics, 2007).

Many students need both—intervention to keep up in the class and remediation to fill in the gaps in their learning. Each school must establish a plan for remediating skills. The plan cannot take students out of direct instruction in the classroom, and it needs to be directly aligned to the students' specific needs. Many schools decide to purchase programs for remediation, but since most students do not have the exact same needs, this is not usually an effective method of remediating all students. In addition, when a student is a grade level or more behind, remediating everything is impossible. Any plan for remediation needs to include only those skills that will accelerate learning in a focused and efficient manner. For example, as mathematics skills are remediated, the instruction too often focuses solely on learning or memorizing addition or multiplication facts. Although mathematics fluency is important, conceptual understanding precedes a student's ability to fluently and efficiently apply operations. Students may need to learn how to compose and decompose numbers to develop flexibility that can be applied to mathematics facts. A student can then realize that $7 + 8$ can be thought of as $7 + 3 + 5$ without having to memorize every sum. Students struggling with mathematics facts can use models and base-ten pieces to develop an understanding of operations with rational numbers to simultaneously learn grade-level content while mathematics fluency is remediated. Students may also need to work on understanding there is more than one way to solve a mathematics problem. Spending a great amount of time on learning the facts is not usually an efficient way to remediate.

Anoka-Hennepin School District in Minnesota looked carefully at the skills and concepts in its elementary mathematics program and determined the most important knowledge that would accelerate student learning. The focus of its remediation is the conceptual understanding of place value because teams realize the impact of grasping this concept has far-reaching implications for understanding mathematics at subsequent grade levels.

This same thinking applies to English language arts remediation. If a student has not learned to read using the traditional phonetic approach, then a different strategy may be necessary. As individual plans for remediating prerequisite skills are developed, the focus needs to be on those specific concepts and skills that accelerate the learning.

Elementary School Remediation

Elementary schools offer remediation in a variety of ways. Some schools create a time block in the schedule so that students will not miss any direct classroom instruction while receiving the additional time and support that they need to be successful. This is often done by grouping students for instruction and giving students who have prerequisite skill deficits a second small-group lesson in addition to their usual small-group work. In some schools, this time block occurs when any additional staff is available to support the students by pushing into the class to do either guided-reading or mathematics groups. Schools implement this expanded-team approach by including any mathematics or reading interventionists, Title I teachers, reading specialists, English as a second language (ESL) teachers, special educators, instructional assistants, librarians, and administrators. In instances where support staff is limited, grade-level teachers share students with like needs to deliver instruction to the second small group. Students are monitored on a weekly basis as the entire expanded team discusses each student's progress. This process harnesses the power within the school and utilizes every resource to ensure all students learn.

When resources are limited in a school, the administration and teachers look for support beyond the school for assistance. Principals actively recruit resources from the community. Some elementary schools organize parent volunteers, business partners, senior citizens, and high school and college interns to serve as mentors and tutors along with the school staff. Schools partner with colleges and universities to be a site for student teachers by offering a location for the university to hold classes for these students at the school or an opportunity to have the principal observe and give formative feedback to the student teacher as she or he teaches a lesson. This serves two purposes: (1) elementary teachers and students gain support from the college students, and (2) schools gain the most effective way to recruit new staff.

Middle School Remediation

Middle schools eliminate one of a student's elective options. In most instances, students have two or three electives in their schedule. Students are placed in a double-blocked course based on achievement indicators. These Academic Achievement courses in reading or mathematics become one of the assigned classes in their schedule. Instruction in these classes follows a preteach-reteach cycle as the gaps in prerequisite skills are filled. As each unit is planned, the Academic Achievement classes preteach the skills and vocabulary for the unit so that students are actually able to participate in the lessons in their regular classes. During the same unit of instruction, the Academic Achievement teachers support the students by scaffolding any foundational or prerequisite concepts necessary to be successful in the unit. After the common assessment is administered in the regular classes, the data are used to reteach any skills and concepts that were not mastered.

In addition, students in the Academic Achievement classes are progress monitored on a weekly or biweekly basis. These results and the data from the regular mathematics and English language arts classes are analyzed to be sure that the time and support the students receive in the second class are not only filling in the gaps in knowledge but also transferring to the course- or grade-level expectations.

High School Remediation

Secondary schools that recognize the need to both remediate and intervene for students often double block students for instruction. High schools create an algebra 1–enhancement class that students take along with the regular algebra 1 course. The second class period is considered an elective credit with the focus on the prerequisite skills necessary to successfully complete algebra 1. The same occurs in English courses. Students who lack the reading skills to be successful in their English course and other content areas are assigned an English-enhancement class along with the usual English class. The enhancement class focuses on reading strategies that ensure students will be able to access the regular curriculum. Comprehension strategies are taught using increasing levels of text complexity.

High school graduation is not a decision; it is a mandate for a better future. Schools create a systematic process that includes the development and monitoring of individual plans for each student that meets the graduation requirements in the most expedient and productive pathway to ensure all students graduate. Strategic individualized student plans contribute to the increased graduation rate. If after careful monitoring and support a senior does not have a chance of graduating based on credits or other requirements no matter how well he or she does during the current school year, then an alternate pathway needs to be instituted. This may mean that the student is redirected to credit recovery, night-school classes in addition to the student's regular classes, alternative school enrollment, general educational development (GED) programs, or any other available options. No student should waste a year without making progress toward graduation in a timely manner. Students who do not graduate with their peers tend to drop out and rarely come back.

Freshmen Academies

The establishment of Freshmen Academies in the school-improvement process proves to be helpful in setting the expectations for graduation early as students enter high school. When implemented successfully, academies build long-term relationships with students and paint a picture of a desirable future for them while clearly articulating the expectations for success. Academies teach the characteristics of a learner necessary for graduation and beyond.

In Freshmen Academies, students are put on teams that include the same four core teachers. These teachers not only meet as content teams but also as a grade-level team. The purpose of grade-level meetings is to monitor student-discipline referrals, absences and tardy incidences, and grades for each student. Teams review attendance, discipline, and grade data to create a watch list of students before they fail. Each team of core teachers develops and implements a plan to intervene for students in one or all of these areas. The intervention plans often include individual student conferences, parent telephone contacts, visits to the home by attendance advocates, counselor support, and joint parent, teacher, and student conferences to develop a plan for school and home.

Tenth-Grade Transition Programs

In some high schools, tenth-grade transition programs follow the Freshmen Academies experience. These programs provide a gradual release of student support in tenth grade and are meant to monitor student progress by teaming mathematics and science teachers together and English and social studies teachers together wherever possible. These combined content-area teams share the same students. This allows similar student-centered discussions to occur as the Freshmen Academy teams engage as well as allows them the opportunity to align content so that students make the connections from course to course.

School improvement requires schools to change the way they do things. The entire school must examine its existing resources—time, people, materials, and money—to provide additional support for *all* students to learn at higher levels than before.

Shifting to a Cycle of Intervention and Extensions for Learning

Interventions are short-term and just-in-time support before students get so far behind that they need remediation. According to DuFour and Mattos (2013), "the key to improved student learning is to ensure more good teaching in more classrooms more of the time" (p. 34). These supports are directly aligned to the learning targets on a unit-by-unit basis. The intent is to support students at the point of need. These short-cycle interventions are a part of first best instruction or daily instruction in every classroom. Meeting the needs of all learners in each classroom is not a solo activity. In a professional learning community, teachers support each other in designing and delivering quality instruction that results in learning for all. Collaborative teams focus on the four PLC questions (page 16) to do this.

Interventions and extensions of learning are planned as grade-level or content teams work collaboratively to answer questions three and four: How will we respond when students do not learn, and How will we respond when they already know it? Just-in-time interventions ensure students keep up with the current level of instruction. Extensions of learning for students who have already learned the targets and standards honor the learning that has occurred and provide meaningful, respectful tasks for students who are ready.

Teams answer these questions together to plan prior to introducing a new unit of instruction. This is a proactive rather than reactive approach to instruction. The most efficient and effective way for teams to do this is to implement an intervention cycle that responds to data from common formative assessments during the unit.

Figure 3.2 outlines a cycle implemented at Northdale Middle School in Minnesota. This cycle guides the teamwork, and the steps in the cycle describe what teams do before, during, and after instruction. Steps one, two, and four are planned before instruction, and steps three and five are addressed after instruction. About two weeks before an upcoming unit of study, teams determine the essential standards that they will teach. They unwrap them to determine the learning targets that underpin the standards. They spend time determining the rigor of the standards by analyzing state-test specifications and released-test items aligned with the standards. They create an assessment plan for the unit that includes the actual format for each common formative assessment and the questions or tasks the students will answer and do. Teams discuss an intervention plan and how they will extend the learning for those students who demonstrate mastery on the assessments.

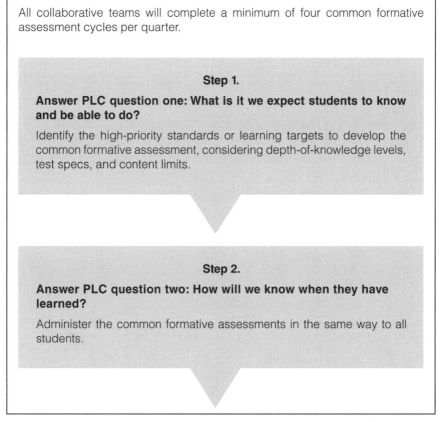

All collaborative teams will complete a minimum of four common formative assessment cycles per quarter.

Step 1.

Answer PLC question one: What is it we expect students to know and be able to do?

Identify the high-priority standards or learning targets to develop the common formative assessment, considering depth-of-knowledge levels, test specs, and content limits.

Step 2.

Answer PLC question two: How will we know when they have learned?

Administer the common formative assessments in the same way to all students.

Continued →

Source: Adapted from Northdale Middle School, Anoka-Hennepin School District, Minnesota. Used with permission.

Figure 3.2: Five easy steps to implementing the intervention cycle.

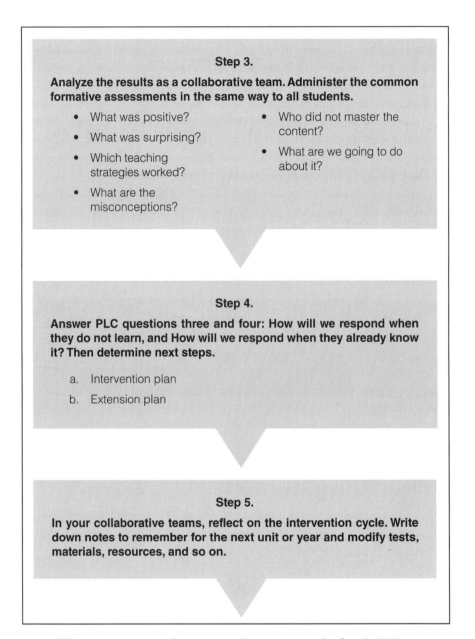

Step 3.

Analyze the results as a collaborative team. Administer the common formative assessments in the same way to all students.

- What was positive?
- What was surprising?
- Which teaching strategies worked?
- What are the misconceptions?

- Who did not master the content?
- What are we going to do about it?

Step 4.

Answer PLC questions three and four: How will we respond when they do not learn, and How will we respond when they already know it? Then determine next steps.

   a. Intervention plan

   b. Extension plan

Step 5.

In your collaborative teams, reflect on the intervention cycle. Write down notes to remember for the next unit or year and modify tests, materials, resources, and so on.

Collaborative teams must be intentional in answering the fourth PLC question. This does not mean that teachers create more work for students. It means that students are engaged in tasks that require them to apply their learning beyond what the teacher taught. Often this can be as simple as engaging students in a singular task. For example, if the learning target is "The student will be able to tell and write time from analog and digital clocks to the nearest five minutes using a.m. and p.m.," the extension task might be to use what was learned to write correct digital time from an analog clock and vice versa. Extending the learning does not require the creation of an entire new unit. Extensions for these students occur at the learning target level and comprise one or two short tasks that can be accomplished while the other students are receiving more direct instruction to learn.

Teams then begin the unit with a shared understanding of the standards and learning targets. They understand the level of rigor necessary for instruction. Teams agree on the proficiency levels the standards require. They have predetermined the possible intervention strategies and extended learning targets and tasks. This proactive process creates a sense of confidence as each teacher approaches the teaching of the concepts and skills.

After the common formative assessments are administered, teams analyze the data using the questions in step three as a guide. They look for common errors and try to understand the reason for the errors. Teachers develop lists of students who need reteaching, more practice, or an extension of learning. In addition, they identify the teaching strategies that were most effective.

Teams plan an additional time block or period the following day to implement the intervention and extension plans that were created before instruction. Teams often share students with like needs for reteaching. If this is not possible, collaborative teams share the work of gathering materials so that every teacher is ready to work with small, flexible groups within their own classroom.

Step five is an opportunity for reflection on the intervention cycle after instruction. Teams approach this as a time to record all the instructional strategies that they want to use the next time they teach this unit. Teachers modify tests, materials, and curriculum resources to better meet the needs of the students. This process represents a recurring cycle on a unit-by-unit basis. This ensures all students are engaged in tasks that specifically meet their needs, whether it is an intervention or an extension of learning. Teams work to make sure all students are keeping up with the curricular demands of the course or grade level. At times, these efforts fall short and then schools look for additional ways to ensure high levels of learning for all students.

Doing Whatever It Takes

In addition to remediation plans and the cycle of interventions already described, improving schools are eager to do whatever it takes to get better achievement for their students. These schools are hungry for data about their students' progress, and they use this information to strategize ways to improve on a continual basis. They are never satisfied with their results. There is an ongoing focus on what to do next. Strategies that have been successful include tutoring programs both during the school day and after school. The tutoring sessions during the school day occur by creating an alternate schedule, much like an activity schedule, on one or two days per week to include a time for students to receive additional instruction while some students participate in extensions of their learning, homework help, or library or computer-lab work. This requires a collective commitment by all staff to *learning for all.*

Additionally, boot camps are held during the school day. This is a designated review the day before the state test, ACT, SAT, or other high-stakes assessment is administered. In tested areas, students are released from their regular schedule to participate in a review of the essential standards on these assessments. Activities and stations for learning are organized so that students work on the standards that they need more help on. Students monitor their own learning by tracking their progress on these priorities so that they know exactly what they need to learn. Teachers work with small groups of students throughout the day to facilitate and instruct at each of the stations.

In some cases, Saturday school is offered. If the school calendar permits, schools use intercessions or breaks in the school year to offer help in failing courses or subjects as well. Teachers call parents to explain why their student needs to attend either of these options and what specifically will be accomplished during this time. The teachers also hold individual or team conferences with students to demonstrate the need to attend.

Finally, collaborative teams develop *triage plans* during the second semester to help students meet the requirements for the next grade level or graduation or the state or national tests. This is usually considered an emergency plan. It is a team approach in that teachers teach all students, not just their own. The team determines the essential standards that need to be retaught and to whom. Since they have collaborative team time during the same period every day and planning time in other time blocks throughout the day, the team trades a collaborative meeting for a planning time so that they can pull students for tutoring in small groups. So instead of meeting daily or three to four times per week, a collaborative team may meet just once or twice per week and use the rest of the time to tutor students. This is only done for a one- to two-month period. All teachers who teach a subject area pull students who need help. This schedule ensures that students receive support all day, not just during the regular collaborative team meeting time.

Two especially important points are: (1) the overarching intent is to create as many options and opportunities for student learning as is reasonably possible, and (2), students should feel as if they are being triple and quadruple teamed and supported to ensure that they learn. The consistent message is this: learning is required here! This message was echoed by the 2012 graduating senior speaker at U.S. Grant High School's graduation ceremony: "You believed in me when I did not believe in myself."

Reflection and Next Steps

Use the following questions to help your team reflect and consider your next steps.

1. How are our school, teams, teachers, and students using data to improve learning? Are we currently doing whatever it takes to improve student achievement in our school?

2. How will we establish a recurring cycle of interventions and extensions that moves learning forward?

3. How will we provide interventions while also remediating prerequisite skills and knowledge? How are we currently remediating student learning? Is there a team plan for interventions and extensions?

4. What options and opportunities exist for the students we serve? What is possible in our school?

Chapter 4

Fourth Challenge: Developing Leadership for Learning

*We've yet to find a single instance in which one talented person . . .
accounted for most, let alone 100%, of the success. You can't do it
alone. Leadership . . . is a team performance . . . The winning strategies will be based on the "we not I" philosophy. Without people we
can't get extraordinary things done in organizations.*

—James M. Kouzes and Barry Z. Posner

There is an urban myth that goes something like this: if a district hires that one
charismatic, brilliant principal, he or she can almost single-handedly turn around
student achievement. Unfortunately, this single factor has never been the sole reason
for higher levels of student achievement. The most adverse myth about leadership is
that it is reserved for only a few individuals. Leadership must be shared and widely
dispersed to realize gains in student achievement. School turnaround can only occur
when the entire school team works together toward a clearly defined vision and
goals. The school must have a strong core of individuals with a moral imperative to
improve student achievement combined with knowledge of all essential elements
needed to reach high levels of student learning for all.

The true definition of leadership is working with others to establish a shared
sense of purpose, goals, and direction and then persuading people to move in that
direction. True leaders clarify the specific steps to be taken to begin moving in the

right direction and provide the resources and support that enables people to succeed at what they are being asked to do.

Another myth is that it takes a special degree in leadership or the completion of a test to be a leader. Over several decades, Kouzes and Posner interviewed people to determine who has had the greatest influence on their lives. It was not surprising that the respondents named parents first and teachers and coaches second. Based on these findings, they state, "If you are in a role that brings you into contact with young people on a regular basis, keep this observation in mind. Someone is looking to you for leadership right now" (Kouzes & Posner, 2010, p. 389).

The fact is that leadership is always a collective endeavor. No one person has all the expertise, skill, and energy to improve a school or meet the needs of every student in his or her classroom. In a professional learning community, instead of being the instructional leader in charge of all things important, the principal becomes the lead learner of the school. In this role, the goal is to build the capacity of the people within the school to ensure high levels of learning for all students. Therefore, improving schools requires widely dispersed leadership and a collective effort.

The school-improvement process is a catalyst for continual change, not first-order change but second-order change or substantive change. This means no amount of tinkering around the edges will result in higher student achievement. Learning for all demands a careful analysis of the current reality of a school compared to best practices followed by actions to improve. It requires everyone to change, not just the people who tend to be early adopters of new ideas. In some instances, change is delayed because it is hard to challenge the status quo. Often no action results in allowing toxic and ineffective practices to remain entrenched.

In their short book *Change Is Good . . . You Go First*, Mac Anderson and Tom Feltenstein (2007) sum up how most people truly feel about change: change is good as long as it does not impact what I do in my classroom. In other words, change struggles to cross the threshold of most classroom doors. Change is really, really hard, and real change is change in the classroom. Leaders of improving schools understand that they cannot make this type of impactful change alone. They know that the most effective way is to share and disperse leadership. Dispersed leadership requires establishing a guiding coalition charged with the responsibility of championing and supporting the process of school improvement. This leadership team, or guiding coalition, supports the work of the teams and teachers. The role is different than the more traditional leadership teams' whose main purpose is to convey information back to their colleagues and provide information to the principal. A guiding coalition works together to lead the work. They represent an alliance of key members of an organization who are specifically charged to lead the change process through the predictable turmoil. Members of this team must have shared goals and high levels of trust. The guiding coalition members are not selected because they have seniority or are current department heads or grade-level leaders. Instead, the key to building a guiding coalition is to start by choosing the right people. Choose people with strong position power, broad experiences, high credibility, and real leadership skills regardless of seniority or current position. Be sure to include opinion leaders because who supports an idea is often more important than the merits of the idea. These leaders are usually socially connected, knowledgeable, and trusted by others. When they are onboard, others usually follow.

Tight and Loose Leadership

Effective leaders of PLCs promote clarity about the work to be done by training and supporting team leaders or facilitators to guide the work of collaborative teams. Leaders empower staff by defining clearly articulated, nondiscretionary parameters and priorities that individuals and teams must adhere to while encouraging them to work in creative and autonomous ways. This means leadership for improvement is both tight *and* loose. Leaders clearly communicate those specific actions and tasks that everyone will do. These are the required, mandated, and expected actions, or tights. No exceptions!

Leaders in improving schools are tight about the following specific actions.

- All teachers work on teams.

- All teachers must contribute to the products of collaboration of their team.

- All teams must establish and monitor SMART goals.

- All teachers teach the agreed-on essential or priority standards.

- All teams create and administer common formative assessments.

- All teachers analyze and use data to intervene and extend student learning.

The tights must be clearly articulated and then monitored through the products of collaboration that are developed as teams work together. Products include SMART goals, common formative and summative assessments, priority standards, unwrapped standards, team agendas, meeting records, data, and intervention and extension plans. (Visit **go.solution-tree.com/PLCbooks** to access the reproducible "PLC Products, Tasks, and Time Lines" to help your team monitor its progress.) An important point to keep in mind in monitoring the tights is what you allow, you promote. Leaders must be willing to confront any and all actions that are not aligned with the mission and do not support the clearly articulated expectations. Leaders undermine the process when they are not willing to confront and redirect individuals or teams whose actions are not aligned with the collective effort to improve student achievement.

Leadership requires both pressure and support. Merely designating the things that are expected without providing the tools, resources, and support results in slow improvement at best. School leaders and teacher leaders know that if they are going to hold others accountable for certain levels of achievement or performance, they must be accountable to them by clarifying the expectations, monitoring team members' progress, and removing obstacles that impede progress while simultaneously providing time, resources, and support. This reciprocal accountability, in addition to providing autonomy for operating within limits at the school site, and the support to nurture success are exactly what improves schools.

In addition, leaders sustain the focus on a limited number of goals and initiatives in order to keep everyone moving toward the singular mission: *learning for all*. As new ideas or initiatives come forward, the guiding coalition asks, "Will this distract from our goal? Will this distract from our mission to improve student learning? Will this further our goal?"

Reflection and Next Steps

Use the following questions to help your team reflect and consider your next steps.

1. How can our school build a leadership structure that supports school improvement?

2. What do we need to do to change the power structure in the school?

3. How can we engage our teachers as leaders?

4. What structures exist to lead and support the teams in PLC work? Is leadership shared and widely dispersed?

5. What are our current initiatives? How many do we have? Are any of the initiatives distracting from the mission of learning for all?

Chapter 5
Fifth Challenge: Engaging Students in Owning Their Learning

Education is not the filling of a pail, but the lighting of a fire.

—William Butler Yeats

Most often, the students in improving schools have not experienced success in learning. They usually are below grade level and struggling to keep up in the curriculum. They are accustomed to getting poor grades and feel like no amount of trying will increase the likelihood that they will be successful. The students who have had repeated failures and know that they are far behind in school often say things like "I can't do math" or "I'm not good at reading or science." Consider this: I walk into a classroom and pose this question to the students: "Mary had a perfect score on her test. Why do you think Mary got 100 percent?" The students will always answer that question with "Because she is smart." In most classrooms, students believe that some students are smart and some are not and that being smart is fixed or cast in stone. Teachers need to help students understand that with effort and preparation, anyone can get the same result as Mary. Carol Dweck (2008) refers to this as the shift from a fixed mindset to a growth mindset. Unfortunately, a growth mindset does not exist in most schools and is particularly absent in failing schools.

As teachers, most of us attended schools that stressed a fixed mindset. So changing to a growth-centered approach may feel a little unnatural. However, our students need to have a reason to come back and try again when they do not do well the first time. Think about this example. A teacher I visited gives her students a twenty-five-point quiz. As she scores the quiz, she notices that one student has missed twenty of the twenty-five questions. This teacher makes a conscious decision to score this quiz differently. Instead of writing "–20" at the top of the paper, she writes "+5" and then adds a smiley face. The student asks, "But isn't this an F?" The teacher's response: "Yes, but you are on a roll! You have five correct, and you are working to get the rest right!" The difference is that an F or –20 is both embarrassing and deflates a student's desire to try again. A +5 and a smiley face indicate that the student is still able to achieve and grow. This is an example of how to foster a growth mindset. This type of approach is important for all students, but it is essential to support struggling students and keep them coming back to engage in the learning process every day.

Engaging students as partners in their learning greatly enhances a growth mindset. This promotes students' self-efficacy and confidence that they can actually reach proficiency and beyond. Since teachers cannot do the work or take the tests for the students in classrooms, partnering with students in the learning process is the way to motivate and engage them. So the real question is, How can we make this happen in every classroom for every student?

Engage Students in Owning Their Learning

Students in today's classroom are poised to take ownership of their learning. Can we agree that the students in classrooms today are members of the Nintendo Wii, Xbox, and PlayStation generation? As they participate in these activities, they clearly understand the concept of beating their own score to reach the next level, and as players, they are highly motivated and engaged. In games, they clearly understand the goal or target and problem solve to reach the next level. They ask others about the codes needed and remember and apply these complex codes as they play. Even those labeled *reluctant readers* or *unmotivated students* persevere over long periods of time to move to the next level. If only we could inspire students to generate the same enthusiasm and perseverance in response to their learning results in the classroom!

The problem may be that these students are often in classrooms taught by adults from the era of more traditional games like *Checkers* and *Monopoly*. Let's examine the differences between traditional and video games, because this may provide some insight as to how the students in today's classrooms think. If we compare video games to traditional games, what are the major differences? How does this impact the way students think?

The answer lies in comparing the responses to the three questions in table 5.1. If you were engaged in playing these games, how would you respond?

This game analogy represents the difference between instructional approaches that are more traditional and teacher centered and the student-centered approach

Table 5.1: Implications of Traditional Versus Video Games for Student Thinking

Questions	Traditional Games	Student Video Games	Implications for Student Thinking
1. Do you need a partner(s)?	Yes	Not necessary but is an option	Students are willing and able to work alone or in groups.
2. Do you have to read and understand the rules?	Yes	Not necessary	Students want to problem solve to the next level.
3. What is the object of the game? How do you win?	Beat the opponent	Get to the next level	Students have a growth mindset!

that is necessary to engage students. In most classrooms, the approach is to tell and demonstrate what students need to know and then offer opportunities to practice the skill or concept. As we examine how students in today's classrooms think, it is evident that they actually learn in a different way when they are engaged in their games. They learn by looking ahead to where they need to get to in the end (highest level or target). Then they determine where they are now as they begin. Finally, they problem solve their way to the next level.

I am not suggesting that teachers implement video games in their classrooms. I am instead suggesting that students from the Nintendo Wii, Xbox, and PlayStation generation may already understand a growth mindset, but the work students do in school does not encourage or capitalize on this thinking. I believe this is a missed opportunity to truly motivate and encourage students. This generation of learners wants and needs to be involved from the start, not just during the practice segment of the lessons.

As students are engaging in playing a video game, they are working hard to get to one more level, one more level, and so on. This is the definition of a growth mindset—the understanding that with effort and preparation, you can get to the next level of learning! This growth mindset is exactly what teachers are trying to accomplish in students as they teach one more standard or learning target. If given the opportunity, the members of this generation are poised to become partners in their learning. This requires that teachers release some of the responsibility for learning to students by clarifying learning targets, providing descriptive feedback, guiding students as they self-assess and set goals, allowing students to support one another in closing learning gaps, having students track their progress, and facilitating student-led conferences. When students engage in their learning and take ownership of the process, they are able to set goals, evaluate their progress, and determine what course of action to take to reach the highest level of achievement. They become motivated, confident partners in their learning.

In his book *Visible Learning: A Synthesis of Over 800 Meta-Analyses Relating to Achievement*, John Hattie (2009) states that student self-reporting of grades and progress has an enormous impact on student achievement. As students track their learning target by target, they are also gaining confidence and watching their advancement one level at a time.

The foundation of student ownership in their learning is a clear understanding of the expectations or learning targets and the ability to envision what would be necessary to achieve this target at the proficient or above level. State standards and learning targets are often written in language that is difficult to understand. So merely writing these standards on the board for students does not help them understand them. In addition, teacher- and team-created, student-friendly versions of the standards may be efficient and helpful, but they alone will not ensure students understand what is expected. Students must envision the end result. They need to answer the question, What will this look like if I do it well? This means that writing it on the board or even telling students the target is not enough. If we want students to clearly understand the target or goal, they need to be engaged in working on understanding the target as the unit of instruction is introduced through questioning techniques, defining concepts in the target that are unfamiliar, or using strategies such as KWL charts. KWL charts ask students to list the information that they think they already know about the topic (K), what they want to learn about it (W), and what they learn as the unit unfolds (L). Another letter, M, can be added for misconceptions. This allows students to move any of the things they thought they knew over as they learn more throughout the unit.

Once students have a clear understanding of the learning targets, they are able to:

- Understand what they know and don't know and their level of achievement

- Plan next steps in their learning

- Fix their work

- Self-assess and set goals
- Keep track of their learning target by target or standard by standard

Tracking knowledge gained learning target by learning target allows students to set realistic goals that help them monitor progress along the way.

Know Your Number

As the learning targets are shared and understood by students, an important part of tracking their learning is to understand where a student is in relation to proficiency. Students determine the gap between where they are now and where they need to be. This allows them to set goals and monitor their progress toward achieving the goals on a target-by-target basis. Teachers have conferences with students to discuss with them the end goal as compared to their current level and to develop a plan with each student to achieve proficiency or above. In other words, the students know their number and are monitoring progress toward getting to the proficient level. Figure 5.1 (page 52) is a sample success plan high school mathematics teachers utilize to develop student learning goals and track progress. In addition to this success plan, the students track the individual learning targets. The information obtained from both the tracking of knowledge gained and the goal allows students to create a plan that is realistic and specific.

In addition to clear learning targets, providing descriptive feedback to students keeps students focused and moves their learning forward. According to Hattie's (2009) synthesis of research on feedback, it is most powerful when the feedback is from the student to the teacher. His research suggests that teachers need to seek out feedback from students about:

- What they know
- What they understand
- Where they have made errors
- When they have misconceptions
- When they are not engaged and why

Most importantly, feedback should cause thinking, not an emotional response. Feedback that moves the learning forward is more work for the recipient than the one giving feedback. It must be targeted and focused on a limited number of targets. This type of feedback leads to more students investing in their learning.

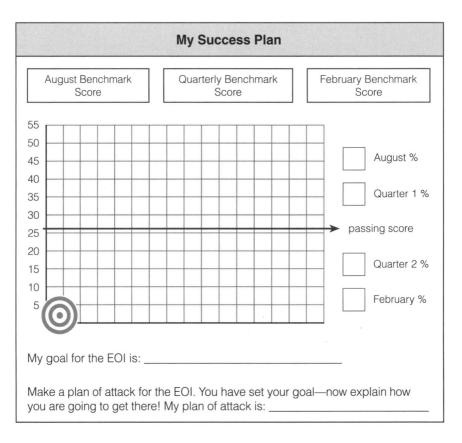

Source: *U.S. Grant High School, Oklahoma City Public Schools, Oklahoma. Used with permission.*

Figure 5.1: U.S. Grant High School end-of-instruction (EOI) assessment.

Apply Strategies That Promote Student Ownership

Student ownership of learning is possible only if the students are continuous partners in the learning process. Strategies that support student involvement in meaningful ways are key to creating a community of student learners in the classroom. Teachers promote engagement when they help students articulate the learning targets in language that they understand. As teachers show examples of strong and weak work, students can envision the targets. Students can also manage their materials and data. Students own their learning when they have data folders and track their progress along the way.

As students track progress, they are also able to set goals based on their current reality and where they need to be. Student goal setting is correlated to greater achievement gains. Students are then able to create plans and action steps to attain their goals. Goal setting is most effective when students can actually see the end. So although long-term goal setting is important and necessary, students are more apt to achieve their goals if there are short-term unit or quarter benchmarks to meet rather than a yearlong goal. The shorter goals promote a growth mindset because celebrations of success are more frequent.

Self-Evaluation

Student engagement also involves students' self-evaluation of their work. Self-assessment is difficult for anyone, but it is especially challenging for students. Often the very bright students are perfectionists and their self-evaluations are underestimations, while students who struggle do not always understand what they do not know yet and have inflated self-evaluations. As students evaluate their progress, they need to use the data they collect as they monitor their learning targets in each unit to determine their strengths and areas of improvement.

Students rarely have an opportunity to reflect on what they have learned and still need to work on. Self-evaluation is powerful because it not only demonstrates the amount of learning that has occurred but also connects each learning experience to the next one. A kindergarten teacher uses the long rolls of butcher paper that typically cover bulletin boards to record what students learn on a daily basis. She draws pictures and writes words as she engages students in describing their learning at the end of each day. On the one hundredth day of kindergarten, she rolls the paper down the school hallway, and students do a learning walk describing to each other all the things that they have learned. This proves to be a powerful example of learning for students and parents.

Teachers at other grade levels and in specific courses at the secondary level are doing the same type of reflection when they ask their students to look through their data notebooks to reflect on their learning on a quarterly basis. As students engage in this activity, the teacher asks them to articulate to a partner how the content is connected one lesson to the next.

Peer Evaluation

Another impactful strategy is to involve students in the peer-evaluation process. Students review each other's work and offer feedback for improvement. This process needs to be structured for students to obtain the best results. Many teachers pair students to review each other's work and indicate *two stars and one wish*. The peer evaluator writes two stars to communicate things that are really good about the work, and one wish conveys something that could be improved. Another activity that requires peer evaluation is the *preflight checklist*. Before students can turn in their assignment to the teacher, they must have one of their peers review their work utilizing a preflight checklist of assignment requirements. This works particularly well when the assignment has specific steps to complete or a rubric to follow, such as in science lab reports or essay writing (Wiliam, 2011).

Finally, utilizing the peer-evaluation process to review homework has proven to be helpful. Often teachers struggle to get students to do homework and turn it in, in a timely fashion. There is a tremendous amount of energy and time focused on the completion of homework when it is difficult to ascertain who actually completed the assignment. An alternative to monitoring homework completion might be to use the peer-evaluation process. Each student is assigned an *accountability buddy*. The students monitor each other's homework completion. They review and discuss wrong answers and offer support and help to each other. Then they turn their work in as a final product. The discussion and support in peer groups usually ensure that the assignment is complete and accurate.

Study Guides

Many teachers develop and distribute study guides before giving an assessment. Study guides can be an effective tool to assist students in learning important content. However, study guides would be more effective if students developed them. So what if a teacher said to students, "We will be putting the study guide together for this unit assessment. I want you to write five questions and their answers, of course, that you believe should be included in the study guide." This activity requires that students actively interact with their text, notes, homework, learning targets, and other resources. As students develop their questions and answers, the teacher is also gathering formative assessment data. If the students do not include the most important concepts from the unit or they include some misconceptions, reteaching may be necessary before administering the assessment. This same process could be utilized to have students generate possible test items.

Student-Led Conferences

Students who own their learning engage in meaningful dialogue about their progress. Many schools participate in student-led conferences with parents. Sometimes these conferences are not as beneficial as they could be because students follow a detailed script during the meeting. This is usually because it is the first time students have been asked to articulate their progress. In order for student-led conferences to be meaningful, students must dialogue about their learning on a continual basis with the teacher, other students, or parents. This type of ongoing student dialogue leads to a greater sense of responsibility and pride in their accomplishments that ultimately results in greater achievement.

Develop Student Leadership for Learning

Developing student leaders is a powerful practice that ensures students are invested in their learning. These are the students who exemplify the learner characteristics that we want all students to embrace. They are students who have achieved proficiency and above and demonstrated growth as learners. The power of positive peer pressure is the key to student motivation and to students' ownership of their learning.

At U.S. Grant High School, the staff developed a Super Seven Seniors group. Members must pass all seven of the end-of-instruction exams the state administers, not just the four that are required. When U.S. Grant instituted the Super Seven Seniors, there were twenty-three students who qualified from a graduating class that totaled 206 students. This group continues to grow and includes 140 students at last count, according to the school administrators. Most importantly, students aspire to be a part of the Super Seven Seniors. They know exactly how many exams they have passed and how many more they need to pass to join the group. They ask their counselors when they can take the exams, often requesting to do this in the early testing window. They are motivated and regularly wear the shirts and medallions that indicate they are a part of this group. The Super Seven Seniors serve as mentors and tutors to the Freshmen Academy students. These positive role models are the new normal at U.S. Grant High School. According to Moss and Brookhart (2009), "Teaching students how to learn, instead of merely what to learn, is valuable work that is worth doing" (p. 151).

Reflection and Next Steps

Use the following questions to help your team reflect and consider your next steps.

1. Do our students have a growth mindset? How can teachers and schools create and foster a growth mindset?

2. What does it take to engage students so that they are partners in the learning process? How can teachers engage students to the extent that they own their learning?

3. As a school, how have we supported the efforts of the teachers and collaborative teams to motivate and engage students?

4. What possibilities exist to increase student investment in the learning process?

Epilogue

So often, schools and districts spend their time looking for that one new thing that is going to result in greater achievement for their students. In their quest to find the key, they adopt new programs and initiatives year after year. Often the number of new initiatives can be overwhelming. Schools and teachers have difficulty keeping up with what is expected of them and often suffer from initiative fatigue. Educators have traditionally been asked to do more and more each year. Teachers want to do all that they can for the students they serve, but the sheer number of initiatives and goals usually paralyzes progress instead of promoting it.

School-improvement efforts must be focused with a limited number of initiatives and new programs. This is difficult given the fact that the students in failing schools often require a great deal of support and help. However, when schools operate as professional learning communities, the mission is clear, and the expectations and actions are focused. The PLC framework guides all the work. As schools become professional learning communities, they are committing to continuous improvement. As such, they organize the entire school into collaborative teams that are focused on the right work that will ensure students learn at high levels. It is not business as usual, and it requires schools to embrace the change process.

I am often asked what the one thing is that improving schools have done to make significant progress. There is no one single defining action that results in school improvement. Instead, improvement requires that teams, teachers, and administrators exert a focused, cohesive, and consistent effort over time. It turns out that school improvement is much like the Flywheel Effect that Jim Collins (2001) describes in *Good to Great: Why Some Companies Make the Leap . . . and Others Don't*:

> The good-to-great companies understood a simple truth: Tremendous power exists in the fact of continued improvement and the delivery of results—however incremental at first—and show how these steps fit into the context of an overall concept that will work. When you do this in a way that people see and *feel* the buildup of momentum, they will line up with enthusiasm. (italics in original, pp. 174–175)

The continuous-improvement process can be characterized more as evolutionary than revolutionary. This means that schools and districts understand that the power is in doing the work of a professional learning community. In the process, each step that is taken pushes the flywheel one inch or two or three until the capacity of the staff is built and you have harnessed the power within.

Now it is your turn. You have examined each challenge and reflected on the implications for your school-improvement efforts. Now it is time to take action and do the work; using figure E.1, answer the following questions: What do you need to start doing to meet each of the challenges? What do you need to stop doing? What specific actions will you take to get the results that your school, teachers, students, and parents desire?

Educators know we can make a difference, and we know it is the right thing to do. I have often heard Rebecca DuFour ask these two questions during her presentations: "If not us, then who? If not now, then when?"

	Start Doing	Stop Doing
First Challenge: Creating a Culture of Success		
Second Challenge: Engaging in the Right Work		
Third Challenge: Shifting From All to Each		
Fourth Challenge: Developing Leadership for Learning		
Fifth Challenge: Engaging Students in Owning Their Learning		

Figure E.1: Start doing–stop doing list.
Visit **go.solution-tree.com/PLCbooks** *for a reproducible version of this figure.*

I believe this anonymous quote describes what it takes to improve schools, "In the end real school improvement requires us to . . . risk more than others think is safe . . . dream more than others think is practical . . . expect more than others think is possible." Professional learning communities are the right work. Improving our schools and increasing the options and opportunities for students change the lives of our students forever.

References and Resources

Ainsworth, L. (2003a). *Power standards: Identifying the standards that matter the most.* Englewood, CO: Lead + Learn Press.

Ainsworth, L. (2003b). *"Unwrapping" the standards: A simple process to make standards manageable.* Englewood, CO: Lead + Learn Press.

American Psychological Association. (2012). *Facing the school dropout dilemma.* Washington, DC: Author. Accessed at www.apa.org/pi/families/resources/school-dropout-prevention.pdf on January 8, 2015.

Anderson, M., & Feltenstein, T. (2007). *Change is good . . . You go first.* Naperville, IL: Simple Truths.

Bailey, K., & Jakicic, C. (2012). *Common formative assessment: A toolkit for professional learning communities at work.* Bloomington, IN: Solution Tree Press.

Black, P., Harrison, C., Lee, C., Marshall, B., & Wiliam, D. (2003). *Assessment for learning: Putting it into practice.* Maidenhead, England: Open University Press.

Black, P., Harrison, C., Lee, C., Marshall, B., & Wiliam, D. (2004). Working inside the black box: Assessment for learning in the classroom. *Phi Delta Kappan, 86*(1), 8–21.

Black, P., & Wiliam, D. (1998). Inside the black box: Raising standards through classroom assessment. *Phi Delta Kappan, 80*(2), 139–148.

Bloom, B. S. (1984). The search for methods of group instruction as effective as one-to-one tutoring. *Educational Leadership, 41*(8), 4–17.

Breslow, J. M. (2012, September 21). By the numbers: Dropping out of high school. *Dropout Nation.* Accessed at www.pbs.org/wgbh/pages/frontline/education/dropout-nation/by-the-numbers-dropping-out-of-high-school on January 8, 2015.

The Broad Foundation. (n.d.). *Our public education system is in deep distress.* Accessed at http://broadeducation.org/about/crisis_stats.html on April 21, 2015.

Buffum, A., Mattos, M., & Weber, C. (2012). *Simplifying response to intervention: Four essential guiding principles.* Bloomington, IN: Solution Tree Press.

Clark, D. L., Lotto, L. S., & Astuto, T. A. (1984). Effective schools and school improvement: A comparative analysis of two lines of inquiry. *Educational Administration Quarterly, 20*(3), 41–68.

Collins, J. (2001). *Good to great: Why some companies make the leap . . . and others don't.* New York: HarperCollins.

DuFour, R. (2011, February 24). *Keynote: Once upon a time—Confronting the mythology of public education.* Presented at the Summit on Professional Learning Communities at Work, Phoenix, AZ.

DuFour, R., DuFour, R., Eaker, R., & Karhanek, G. (2004). *Whatever it takes: How professional learning communities respond when kids don't learn.* Bloomington, IN: Solution Tree Press.

DuFour, R., DuFour, R., Eaker, R., & Karhanek, G. (2010). *Raising the bar and closing the gap: Whatever it takes.* Bloomington, IN: Solution Tree Press.

DuFour, R., DuFour, R., Eaker, R., & Many, T. (2010). *Learning by doing: A handbook for professional learning communities at work* (2nd ed.). Bloomington, IN: Solution Tree Press.

DuFour, R., & Mattos, M. (2013). How do principals really improve schools? *Educational Leadership, 70*(7), 34–40.

Dweck, C. S. (2008). *Mindset: The new psychology of success.* New York: Ballantine Books.

Eaker, R., & Keating, J. (2012). *Every school, every team, every classroom: District leadership for growing professional learning communities at work.* Bloomington, IN: Solution Tree Press.

Greenstone, M., Looney, A., Patashnik, J., & Yu, M. (2013, June). *Thirteen economic facts about social mobility and the role of education.* Washington, DC: Brookings Institution. Accessed at www.brookings.edu/research/reports/2013/06/13-facts-higher-education on January 8, 2015.

Hattie, J. (2009). *Visible learning: A synthesis of over 800 meta-analyses relating to achievement.* New York: Routledge.

Haun, G. (2009). *Reflections of Helen: An analysis of the words and wisdom of Helen Keller.* Bloomington, IN: AuthorHouse.

Kouzes, J. M., & Posner, B. Z. (2003). *Credibility: How leaders gain and lose it, why people demand it.* San Francisco: Jossey-Bass.

Kouzes, J. M., & Posner, B. Z. (2007). *The leadership challenge* (4th ed.). San Francisco: Jossey-Bass.

Kouzes, J. M., & Posner, B. Z. (2010). *The truth about leadership: The no-fads, heart-of-the-matter facts you need to know.* San Francisco: Jossey-Bass.

Lickona, T., & Davidson, M. (2005). *Smart & good high schools: Integrating excellence and ethics for success in school, work, and beyond—Promising practices for building 8 strengths of character that help youth lead productive, ethical, an fulfilling lives* (A report to the nation). Cortland: Center for the 4th and 5th Rs (Respect and Responsibility) State University of New York College at Cortland.

Marzano, R. J. (2003). *What works in schools: Translating research into action.* Alexandria, VA: Association for Supervision and Curriculum Development.

Marzano, R. J. (2007). *The art and science of teaching: A comprehensive framework for effective instruction.* Alexandria, VA: Association for Supervision and Curriculum Development.

Moss, C. M., & Brookhart, S. M. (2009). *Advancing formative assessment in every classroom: A guide for instructional leaders.* Alexandria, VA: Association for Supervision and Curriculum Development.

National Council of Teachers of Mathematics. (2007). *Creating or selecting intervention programs.* Accessed at http://old.nctm.org/uploadedFiles/Lessons _and_Resources/Intervention_Resources/Intervention%20Programs%20 %28NCTM,%20Nov%202007%29.pdf on April 21, 2015.

National Governors Association Center for Best Practices & Council of Chief State School Officers. (2010). *Common Core State Standards for English language arts and literacy in history/social studies, science, and technical subjects.* Washington, DC: Authors. Accessed at www.corestandards.org/assets/CCSSI_ELA%20Standards .pdf on January 8, 2015.

The Oklahoman Editorial Board. (2012, March 6). *Delaying new graduation tests won't serve Oklahoma high school students.* Accessed at http://newsok.com/delaying-new -graduation-tests-wont-serve-oklahoma-high-school-students/article/3654873 on March 2, 2015.

Organisation for Economic Co-operation and Development. (2009). *Education at a glance 2009: OECD indicators.* Paris: Author.

Organisation for Economic Co-operation and Development. (2011). *Editorial: Fifty years of change in education.* Accessed at www.oecd.org/dataoecd/37/45/48642586 .pdf on January 8, 2015.

Reardon, S. F. (2011). The widening academic achievement gap between the rich and the poor: New evidence and possible explanations. In G. J. Duncan & R. J. Murnane (Eds.), *Whither opportunity?: Rising inequality, schools, and children's life chances* (pp. 91–116). New York: Russell Sage Foundation.

Scherer, M. (2001). How and why standards can improve student achievement: A conversation with Robert J. Marzano. *Educational Leadership, 59*(1), 14–18.

Sparks, S. D. (2013, July 29). Dropout indicators found for 1st graders. *Education Week.* Accessed at www.edweek.org/ew/articles/2013/07/29/37firstgrade.h32 .html?tkn=YRXFxf2U7fneiq Zz7tQQsojrJgXCEYZRzZxk&cmp=ENL-EU -NEWS1 on January 8, 2015.

Tavernise, S. (2012, February 9). Education gap grows between rich and poor, studies say. *The New York Times*, p. A1. Accessed at www.nytimes.com/2012/02/10 /education/education-gap-grows-between-rich-and-poor-studies-show .html?pagewanted=all on January 8, 2015.

United States Census Bureau. (2006). *Current population survey: Educational attainment in the United States*. Washington, DC: U.S. Department of Commerce.

Wiliam, D. (2011). *Embedded formative assessment*. Bloomington, IN: Solution Tree Press.

Solutions for Professional Learning Communities

The *Solutions Series* offers practitioners easy-to-implement recommendations on each book's topic—professional learning communities, digital classrooms, or modern learning. In a short, reader-friendly format, these how-to guides equip K–12 educators with the tools they need to take their school or district to the next level.

How to Use Digital Tools to Support Teachers in a PLC
William M. Ferriter
BKF675

How to Leverage PLCs for School Improvement
Sharon V. Kramer
BKF668

How to Coach Leadership in a PLC
Marc Johnson
BKF667

How to Develop PLCs for Singletons and Small Schools
Aaron Hansen
BKF676

How to Cultivate Collaboration in a PLC
Susan K. Sparks and Thomas W. Many
BKF678

How to Launch PLCs in Your District
W. Richard Smith
BKF665

> # Tremendous, tremendous, tremendous!
>
> The speaker made me do some very deep internal reflection about the **PLC process** and the personal responsibility I have in making the school improvement process work **for ALL kids.**

—Marc Rodriguez, teacher effectiveness coach,
Denver Public Schools, Colorado

PD Services

Our experts draw from decades of research and their own experiences to bring you practical strategies for building and sustaining a high-performing PLC. You can choose from a range of customizable services, from a one-day overview to a multiyear process.

Book your PLC PD today!
888.763.9045

Solution Tree